Wallace Bruce

The Lincoln Monument,

in memory of Scottish-American soldiers, unveiled in Edinburgh, August

21, 1893

Wallace Bruce

The Lincoln Monument,
in memory of Scottish-American soldiers, unveiled in Edinburgh, August 21, 1893

ISBN/EAN: 9783337243395

Printed in Europe, USA, Canada, Australia, Japan

Cover: Foto ©ninafisch / pixelio.de

More available books at **www.hansebooks.com**

THE

LINCOLN MONUMENT

IN MEMORY OF

SCOTTISH-AMERICAN SOLDIERS

UNVEILED IN EDINBURGH

AUGUST 21, 1893

PRINTED BY

WILLIAM BLACKWOOD AND SONS

EDINBURGH: MDCCCXCIII

WALLACE BRUCE HOME AGAIN.

Hon. WALLACE BRUCE returns to New York after four years' absence as United States Consul at Edinburgh. As his friends at home and abroad know, he has won golden opinions in Great Britain as a lecturer, poet, orator, and a man of business. We welcome him again to the Lecture platform. Although he proposes to give more time to literature in the future, we are pleased to know that he will accept a limited number of engagements during the autumn and early winter, before going to his winter home at De Funiak Springs, Florida.

The following pages present an account of Mr Bruce's latest achievement in erecting a Monument of Lincoln in Edinburgh, "in Memory of Scottish-American Soldiers." Also, the esteem of the citizens among whom he has lived for four years as an American representative.

We are gratified to present the following illustrations connected with the day's proceedings :—

THE LINCOLN MONUMENT.
MISS BRUCE UNVEILING MEMORIAL.
AFTER THE UNVEILING.
THE LOVING-CUP.

LECTURE SUBJECTS FOR 1893-94.

SCOTTISH SHRINES (*New*).

THE STORY OF SHAKESPEARE (*New*).

THE HAUNTS OF BURNS (*New*).

WIT AND HUMOR.

WOMANHOOD IN SHAKESPEARE.

CHILDHOOD IN DICKENS.

LANDMARKS OF SCOTT.

For Terms and Dates, address—

BRYANT LITERARY UNION,

53 EVENING POST BUILDING,

NEW YORK.

UNVEILING

OF THE

MEMORIAL TO SCOTTISH-AMERICAN SOLDIERS.

—————◆—————

(The descriptive matter in the following pages is taken from the 'Scotsman' and the 'Scottish Leader': the addresses from steno-graphic report and speakers' notes.)

THE memorial to Scottish-American soldiers, which has been subscribed for by American citizens, primarily through the instrumentality of Hon. Wallace Bruce, United States Consul, Edinburgh, was unveiled yesterday afternoon in the Old Calton Burying-Ground. Outside the gates a large crowd gathered by four o'clock. Keen was the anxiety to gain admittance to the ancient cemetery, but only those provided with cards of admission were permitted to ascend the stair-way. On the old Calton Hill, and at the Waterloo Place windows, were many spectators, who could witness the ceremony, although debarred from hearkening to the speeches. The arrival of the band, pipers, and guard of honor, some 250 strong, of the Argyll and Sutherland Highlanders, was the first event of importance. Under the command of Captain Cavendish, the men, with band and pipers playing alternately, had marched from the Castle by way of the Mound and Waverley Bridge. There was a very large assemblage of those invited. The monument, draped in the Stars and Stripes and the Union Jack, stood a few paces to the northward of the plain circular tower commemorating David Hume, the historian. Near by was erected a convenient platform. It was decorated with three banners—the Stars and Stripes, the Union Jack, and the Scottish Standard, and there was an edging of heather along the platform front. Round this the soldiers formed, and the spectators pressed behind the Highlanders. There were many visitors from across the Atlantic, and the half-hour's wait amid so many reminiscences of the Scottish past would under better weather conditions have been spent with interest. The Old Calton graveyard contains many stone links with former times, and the most prominent is the massive obelisk raised in honor of the political martyrs of 1794—Muir, Palmer, Skirving, Gerrald, and Margarot, who were banished the country for their political opinions. Unfortunately the weather was not of the best, a boisterous south-west wind, which had been blowing all day, being accompanied by showers of rain just as the time arrived for the commencement of the interesting proceedings. From its elevated position on the Calton rock the burying-ground was swept by the blast, and umbrellas were of little use. Precisely at half-past four the platform company made their appearance. The Lord Provost, Bailies, and Councillors were in full robes of scarlet and white, and were attended by the city officials. Lieutenant-General Lyon-Fremantle, Commanding the Troops in Scotland; Captain Ewart, his aide-de-camp; and Colonel Hannay, of the Highlanders, were in uniform. The Chairman was Sir William Arrol, who had on his right Hon. Wallace Bruce, the Lord Provost, General Fremantle, and on his left Bailies Walcot and Macpherson. Amongst those present were — Councillors Cranston, Pollard, Mortimer, Eunson, Telfer, Scott, and Murray; Mr Skinner, Town-Clerk; and Mr Morham, City Architect; Sir Charles Dalrymple, Bart., M.P.; Rev. Professor Christie, D.D., Pennsylvania; Mr Geo. E. Bissell, sculptor; Mr Henry R. Heath, New York, Chairman of Monument Committee; Hon. Allen B. Morse, United States Consul at Glasgow; Miss Bruce and Miss Burton.

The Unveiling.

After the National Anthem, and Dedicatory Prayer by Rev. Professor Christie of Pittsburg, Pa., and brief addresses by Sir William Arrol, Chairman of the day, and by Mr Henry R. Heath of New York, Chairman of Committee, Miss Bruce, attired in a flowing white costume, and having her hair encircled in a band of gold—representing Columbia—drew a cord, which removed the British and American flags that had hitherto veiled the monument. Upon the memorial being exposed to view, a loud cheer burst from the assemblage, and the band of the Highlanders played " Hail Columbia " and " Rule Britannia." Hearty calls were raised for the sculptor, who came to the front of the platform and bowed his acknowledgments. His work, it is the barest justice to say, was very greatly admired.

Cablegram from the Hon. Chauncey M. Depew.

NEW YORK, *August 3*, 1893.

WALLACE BRUCE,
United States Consul, Edinburgh.

Have been compelled to change plans. Deeply regret that I cannot come.   CHAUNCEY M. DEPEW.

MISS BRUCE UNVEILING MEMORIAL.

Presentation Address by Hon. Wallace Bruce, U.S. Consul.

Hon. WALLACE BRUCE, on rising to formally hand over the memorial to the custody of the Corporation of Edinburgh, was received with loud applause. He said — Sir William Arrol, my Lord Provost, Magistrates, and Town Council of Edinburgh, ladies and gentlemen, it was expected until a few days ago that Honorable Chauncey M. Depew, the prince of American orators, would grace this occasion. Unavoidable circumstance has prevented him. I know how his genial eloquence would have stirred the warm Scottish heart. Taking his place here to-day, I come with no carefully studied sentences, but with a few notes sketched during a busy week, hoping thereby to voice the emotion and the feeling of this assemblage. There are two ideas, I take it, uppermost in the hearts of the people here gathered—the struggle for freedom, and the martyrdom of its heroes. (Applause.) On the base of this monument just unveiled are the noble words of the martyred President—" TO PRESERVE THE JEWEL OF LIBERTY IN THE FRAMEWORK OF FREEDOM." (Hear, hear.) This is the condensation of all history, from Marathon and Platæa to the last struggle for human rights.

We measure time by glorious deeds,
   All history is simply this :
It skips the years ; it merely reads
   From Marathon to Salamis.

(Applause.) He reads history to little advantage who
sees only a succession of detached and doubtful battles.
He is the true philosophic historian who sees the course
of Providence on every battle-field, and in the halls of
our legislation. (Hear, hear.) He who traces the
torch of liberty from country to country, from century
to century, from generation to generation—he sees it
flash over the hills of Judæa, across the plains of Marathon, through the mountain-passes of Switzerland, by
the dykes of Holland, along the shores of Loch Lomond
and the Links of Forth, where men struggled for liberty,
for human rights and independence. (Applause.) Republic after republic has passed away, monarchy after
monarchy has given place to new succession, but the
course of individual liberty has been onward and up-
ward—the struggle to give liberty to the individual and
freedom to the State. This is the epitome of the history of Britain. Forces for one thousand years have
struggled here in this island home. The Saxon, the
Gael, the Norman, have furnished the yeast of civilisation, and their descendants nurtured here have carried it all over the world. (Hear, hear.) I stood a

short time ago among the mountains of Saxon-Switzer-
land, and, as I looked at the river Elbe flowing down to
the sea, I thought of the rock-fibre worn away through
the ages, carried westward by its waters, bearing on
toward your shores the enduring sediment of Saxon
freedom wrought out in those old German forests.
(Applause.)

This island seems to have been set apart by Providence to transmit this individual liberty to all
generations. You have an interesting custom, annu-
ally celebrated in many towns and burghs of your
country, of Riding the Marches. Tell me where to-day
are the marches of Great Britain? Despatch your
swiftest ships to the five hundred red-dotted islands
of the globe. Visit Australia, New Zealand, India,
Canada. Where are the marches of the English
language? (Applause.) Is it not the marvel of the
world—ay, the marvel of civilisation—that this com-
pact island, gathering up within herself these elements,
should have done so much to make sure the cause of
freedom? (Applause.) The Atlantic, to-day, is nar-
rower than yonder Forth three centuries ago. Think
of those who would have had a message then to send
from Edinburgh to the hills of Fife, or of those
who, to-day, speak in a single moment to New York
or San Francisco. The widest ocean in the world

is the English Channel. Why? Because you must needs translate your telegraphic and telephonic utterance into foreign speech twenty miles from your coast. The Atlantic cable to-day carries a language unchanged all round the globe. Bulwer says —"All war is a misunderstanding." There can be no misunderstanding among peoples, and the nations will learn war no more, when the English language proclaims its final mission of universal brotherhood. (Applause.) British history, my friends, is near to the American heart. We stand among the ruins of continental Europe with reverence. We come and stand here among your shrines with love. Each castle which sentinelled your hill-tops was a school-house for our ancestors. The school-house to-day is the castle of posterity. (Applause.)

We are celebrating across the sea the four-hundredth anniversary of the Discovery of America. Is it too much to say that Columbus waited for John Wycliff, or that the Mayflower waited for Shakespeare? Britain was to be the threshold to the great Continent. The old legend of the giant stepping from Scotland to Ailsa Craig, to Rathlin Isle, and so to Ireland, has been more than realised. The giants of Britain in intellect —your Macaulays, your Humes, your Blackstones, your Miltons—have strided in giant-like marches from every

crag of Britain to the farthermost stones of the Sierra
Nevadas. Some time ago I had the honor of giving
an address on Scottish literature in the good old town
of Ayr. Sir William Arrol was in the chair, and I
called to mind the fact that when a suspension-bridge
was thrown over the gorge of Niagara, a kite was sent
across first. The kite bore a cord, the cord a rope, the
rope a cable, until a bridge spanned the channel. I
said that Sir William Arrol in his Forth Bridge had
built the greatest except one in the world, and that was
a bridge of light that spanned the Atlantic : that when
the wind blew from the east, it took the kites of Shakespeare, of Shelley, of Byron, of Scott, and of Burns ;
and that when the wind was from the west, it took the
kites of Longfellow, of Whittier, of Bryant, of Holmes,
and of Lowell, until the threads were woven together,
and a great choral bridge joined the English world.
(Applause.) Some of our struggles in America have
been the inheritance of our ancestors. The civil war
was one of these. We had to fight out the battles of
those ideas that we were evolving from it just when
our States after the Revolution formed themselves into
one nation. This monument in memory of Scottish
soldiers is a tribute to brave men who fought there for
freedom. I recall a monument to Lord Chatham in
Charleston, South Carolina. I think of the Scotch-

Puritan fathers who went from the Trossachs to our Blue Ridge mountains—men who formed the Mecklenburg Declaration that preceded American Independence. I have stood, my friends, in Euchee Anna, near the shore of the crystal lake of De Funiak Springs in Florida, and read upon a monumental shaft the names of the Campbells, and descendants from dear old Scotland, who went into the war fighting for what they considered their right and their duty. And to-day there is no feeling but love across any line or between any State. The Saxon blood is well knit there. I see men in this gathering here who were on different sides of this war. They know the stubborn gallantry of the Anglo-Saxon race. I have heard the battle of Gettysburg described. Perhaps the grandest charge in the world's history was when Pickett moved across that field, doomed to death by artillery from commanding hill-tops; but on, still on, up to the very jaws of flaming cannon, bayonet to bayonet, army against army. Ah, my friends, there was equal bravery, but God was on the side of the Republic of America! (Applause.) Our great country, bound together by its rivers and its mountain-chains, was to remain inseparable for all time. (Applause.)

We have a happy location for this monument— the first ever erected to Lincoln in Europe—in the most beautiful city of the world. What associations! Arthur's Seat and Salisbury Crags. Yonder Castle, with its history of one thousand years; the Gothic monument of Sir Walter Scott; the noble Forth, tossed by storm or sleeping in sunlight; the old High Street, with its marvellous associations,—what a realm of history and romance, what a wonderful city! (Hear, hear.) We are, moreover, proud to have it here in your historic burial-ground, associated with memories of Walter Scott and of Robert Burns. Over there is the memorial of the representative of Bailie Nicol Jarvie; a little farther to the right the unmarked grave of Willie Nicol, with whom Burns lived in Edinburgh. There sleep the Constables, the publishers of Scott's novels. There one of the five " Belles of Mauchline," mother of Dr Candlish, the great preacher, cradled again by his mother's couch. Here the monument to David Hume, whose death followed closely upon the Declaration of Independence; and yonder obelisk—the People's Monument—erected to those who struggled for a wider suffrage, to Muir, Palmer, Skirving, Margarot, and Gerrald, exiled in the cause of liberty. "It is a good cause. It shall ultimately prevail. It shall finally triumph," said Muir. "I know," says Skirving, "that what has been done these two days will be rejudged." We celebrate to-day—the very centenary of that utterance—by unveiling a monument to the last great martyr in the cause of Saxon freedom—an honest man, who saved us in the hour of our peril. May it stand to all time as a memorial to your heroes who fought for their adopted home beyond the sea—as a resting-place for those who have returned, and have no shelter in the last hour, and as another bond of widening love and friendship between Great Britain and the United States of America. (Great applause.)

Mr Wallace Bruce concluded his eloquent address by reading a formal minute of the Committee of Arrangements requesting the Lord Provost, Magistrates, and Council to accept custody of the Memorial.

The LORD PROVOST said—Sir William Arrol, Mr Wallace Bruce, ladies and gentlemen—I have great pleasure, on behalf of the Town Council of Edinburgh, in accepting the custody of this monument, which speaks of so many things at one time. Seeing that the weather is so inclement, I should have been very glad indeed to have followed the example of Mr Wallace Bruce in leaving the poem which was to have concluded his oration to readers of this day's proceedings, and confided what I had to say to the press in written manuscript. (Laughter.) But, alas! I am making a reply, and I have only two or three pencilled notes and cannot adopt that expedient. There are many reasons, which you can easily divine, why we rejoice to accept the custody of this monument. It is a monument to our countrymen who were engaged in a memorable struggle —a struggle which proved a crisis in the history of the Anglo-Saxon race on the American continent. It is a monument to freedom, and we are glad that we have been able to give a site for this monument in a burial-place where there are other monuments to men who did great things in procuring liberty and freedom. I have just been informed that these proceedings to-day partake not only of an international character, but remind us Scotch people of a struggle for freedom in which we were engaged. The American clergyman who opened the proceedings here with prayer, was born on the memorable field of Bannockburn in Scotland. (Applause.) We also accept gratefully the custody of this monument as an act of courtesy and friendship to the United States of America. We are deeply interested in the United States ; we are materially interested in the United States; we are morally interested in the United States. We owe them a great debt of gratitude for helping us on in the path of freedom, and by showing us an example of freedom, helping those who were struggling for freedom in this country. With their great influence they have done a

B

great deal to help us in becoming freer than we were in the past. The presence here of the gentleman commanding the army in Scotland, and its officers and soldiers, speaks of itself as a greeting to their comrades in arms in the United States. (Applause.) And I feel that in the inauguration of this monument in Edinburgh and in this burial-place, we have established another object of interest, which must for long years to come attract numerous pilgrims from across the Atlantic. Edinburgh is, as has been said, rich in historic memories. It is rich in memories of great men and of their works, and we are proud to see so many of our kinsmen from across the sea coming here to claim their patrimony in our history, to claim their right to share in our common history, and to admire the objects which remind us of the great events in the common history of the two countries. And I feel, as I have said, that we have now got another attraction for those persons in the possession of this monument within our city. I have the greatest pleasure, therefore, on behalf of the Town Council of Edinburgh, in accepting the custody of this monument; and I can promise you, sir, that we shall guard it carefully and see that it suffers no loss. (Loud applause, following which the band of the Highlanders played " Auld Langsyne.")

AFTER THE UNVEILING.

Lieutenant-General LYON-FREMANTLE, C.B., said—I have to propose a vote of thanks to Sir William Arrol for having presided on such an occasion. I am sure our friends in America will appreciate the fact of so great and good a man presiding upon an occasion of this sort. (Applause.)

Mr WALLACE BRUCE said—I have the pleasure of proposing a vote of thanks to General Lyon-Fremantle for honoring us with his presence, attended by officers and soldiers of the Argyll and Sutherland Regiment, accompanied by the Castle band, who have graced this occasion, thereby contributing so much to this imposing ceremony. (Applause.)

Sir WILLIAM ARROL, in returning thanks, said—It has been a very great pleasure to me to come here to-day. I think the people of Edinburgh ought to be proud of this handsome monument, erected by Americans in this historic city. I am sure that the people who come here for their annual pilgrimage will view this beautiful monument with great satisfaction. (Hear, hear.)

The proceedings then terminated.

COLUMBIA'S GARLAND.

By WALLACE BRUCE.

AT THE UNVEILING OF THE LINCOLN MONUMENT IN EDINBURGH,
IN MEMORY OF SCOTTISH-AMERICAN SOLDIERS.

A NOTHER clasp of loving hands,
  Another link across the sea,
A living word from distant lands
  To grace the soldiers of the free ;
    Columbia, at her Mother's knee,
    Unfolds the scroll of Liberty.

A parchment born of bitter years,
  Red-lined with blood of martyrs leal,
Dark-stained and blurred by captives' tears,
  By dungeon-mould and rusted steel—
    A charter sealed beneath the star
    That led the nations from afar ;

To find a green-girt island home,
  With moat outlasting gates of steel,
Whose bulwark was the ocean foam,
  Whose drawbridge was the floating keel,
    Whereon to bear all round the world
    The flag of Destiny unfurled.

Your Magna Charta rode secure
　　Within the Mayflower's narrow hold,
That invoice made the shipment sure—
　　A Britain poured in larger mould ;
　　　Your Gaelic-Saxon-Norman blood—
　　　The yeast of Time's great brotherhood

What complex forces strangely wrought,
　　What lasting victories nobly won,
Since Sidney died and Hampden fought,
　　Or Milton dreamed of Washington :
　　　Virginia voiced your living creed—
　　　A scion true of Runnymede.

With tendrils reaching west to rear
　　The highest type of manhood's power
Born of the soil, without a peer,
　　Our Lincoln stands the noblest flower
　　　Of freedom in its widening course
　　　From Chatham, Fox, and Wilberforce :

To whom an anxious nation turned
　　When gathering clouds the sky o'ercast,
A pilot brave with soul that yearned
　　To guide the ship before the blast ;
　　　To hold the faith our fathers knew,
　　　To keep the stars within the blue.

A genius stamped with sterling worth,
　　Despising juggling and pretence,
His story halos humble birth,
　　A parable of modest sense ;
　　　Endowed to see and do the right—
　　　The Majesty of moral might.

Inspired to set in simple speech
  The words that sway a people's heart.
Prophetic sentences that reach
  Beyond the realm and scope of art;
    The humor of a nation's youth,
    The wit of plain and homely truth.

'Twas this upheld the faltering arm,
  When hearts were faint and bowed in prayer;
His honest face had power to charm
  And ease the burden of our care;
    With will serene that masters fate,
    He taught the land to trust and wait.

With bended knee and listening ear
  He watched the hour to speak and save;
Hark! Bells peal out an anthem clear—
  He strikes the shackle from the slave:
    That deed completes the work begun
    By Jefferson and Hamilton.

Embodied here to stand for aye
  In memory of soldiers brave,
Who stood in many a bloody fray
  In serried ranks our land to save;
To Scotia's sons we proudly turn—
  Descendants true of Bannockburn.

We cannot consecrate this ground,
  No deed of ours the debt can pay;
The ray across each martyr's mound
  Gets stronger purchase day by day—
    Each soldier's grave a fulcrum sod—
    The lever in the hand of God;

To lift the world to larger life,
　To loftier dreams and nobler deeds,
To broaden faith and narrow strife,
　To plant the rose and crush the weeds,
　　Till jealousies forget their date—
　· The worn-out cerements of hate.

Through prismed tears let sunlight play,
　Secure in joy, redeemed in grief;
One song unites the Blue and Gray,
　One glory binds the garnered sheaf—
　　War's cruel reaping kindly sealed
　　By brothers of the martyred field.

And so Columbia comes with cheer,
　With outstretched hand from o'er the sea,
To place a garland on the bier
　Of those who died to keep us free;
　　And here, beside her Mother's knee,
　　Unfolds the scroll of Liberty.

FAREWELL TO HON. WALLACE BRUCE.

PRESENTATION OF LOVING-CUP

FROM TOWN COUNCIL, IN THE COUNCIL CHAMBERS, BEFORE THE
UNVEILING OF MONUMENT.

YESTERDAY Mr Wallace Bruce must have realised
what it is to have one crowded hour of glorious
life—that is, if congratulatory speeches and farewell
honors are a cause of happiness. The presentation
to him of a Loving-cup by the municipality was a high
and unusual token of regard, rendered the more interesting as to the form of it by the reminiscences of
a time when loving-cups were more cherished and
oftener in use. The unveiling of the Lincoln Memorial
was a ceremony that had the secondary interest of
marking the close of Mr Bruce's official career amongst
us; and the dinner in the evening was a great occasion of good feeling and of eloquence.

The presentation was made by Lord Provost Russell
in the Council Chambers, where a large and representative gathering assembled to do honour to Mr Wallace
Bruce, both in his public capacity and as a personal
friend. The company included most of the members

THE LOVING-CUP.

of the Corporation, several leading citizens, and a number of American ladies and gentlemen, both resident in the city and sojourning for a brief period. On the right of the Lord Provost were Mr Wallace Bruce, Mrs Bartlett, Mr Peacock, American Vice-Consul, and Mr J. Wilson Shiels; and on the left Mrs Wallace Bruce, Mr W. E. Bartlett, Mr Henry R. Heath, New York; Bailie Walcot, and Bailie Macpherson.

The Corporation's gift was a handsome solid silver loving-cup of the old Scotch pattern, weighing seventy-five ounces. The three handles were represented by modelled thistles, the leaves of which afforded a good grip of the goblet. The border was also composed of thistles richly chased in *repoussé* work, and the feet were represented by eagle's claws, with a spray of thistles forming an ornament on the cup. On one section of the cup were inscribed the following words :—

PRESENTED TO

HON. WALLACE BRUCE,

CONSUL OF THE UNITED STATES OF AMERICA,

BY THE

LORD PROVOST, MAGISTRATES, AND TOWN COUNCIL
OF EDINBURGH,

ON HIS RETIRING FROM OFFICE IN THE CITY,

AS A MARK OF ESTEEM, AND RECOGNITION

OF

HIS SERVICES TO SCOTTISH LITERATURE.

SEPTEMBER 1893.

The LORD PROVOST, in opening the proceedings, said—
Ladies and gentlemen, we are called together here
to-day on an occasion which is at once joyous and
painful. We are assembled to do honor to a gentleman who has occupied a prominent position among
us, and at the same time to say good-bye to him in
his official capacity. You know that our friend, the
American Consul, Mr Wallace Bruce—(applause)—
demits office on the 1st September, and this is his
formal good-bye to the Town Council of Edinburgh.
We have been fortunate in this country in the ambas-
sadors and consuls sent to us by the United States.
They have had the wisdom to send, in many cases,
literary men of great distinction, and we feel grateful to
the United States for having sent to us, in Mr Wallace
Bruce, not only a literary man, but a man whose name
proclaims his Scottish origin. (Applause.) While with
us he has joined in our intellectual life.   His voice
and pen have always been ready at the call of the
citizens, either in the cause of charity or in the cause
of social reunions, and he has achieved for himself a
degree of popularity which rarely falls to the lot of
one who has only a limited sojourn in the town.   I
believe that his work as a consul has been well done.
We have had, however, consuls from the United States
in Edinburgh who have done their work just as well, so

far as looking after business affairs was concerned ; but there is a much higher distinction that Mr Wallace Bruce has achieved among us. He has helped to keep alive on both sides of the Atlantic the memory of our great men of the past. He has, still more, helped to bring to the vision of ordinary people the very real personages who never existed in the flesh, but yet throng the historic streets of Edinburgh. (Applause.) He has himself contributed several rills to the stream of Scottish literature, and he has endeavoured—and this is a very practical and serious claim upon our regard in every way—to promote a kindly feeling between kinsmen of the two countries separated by the Atlantic Ocean, and has sought to mix " the Clover with the Heather." (Applause.) The Town Council could not part with such a man without showing him some official mark of their approbation and esteem— (applause)—and we have therefore agreed to ask his acceptance of a loving-cup, as a small acknowledgment of his services among us. (Applause.) I have now the pleasure, in the name of the Corporation, of asking Mr Bruce's acceptance of this small tangible token of our esteem for him personally, and recognition of his grateful services while Consul among us. (Loud applause, amid which the loving-cup, which was greatly admired, was handed to Mr Wallace Bruce.)

Mr WALLACE BRUCE, who was cordially received, said—My Lord Provost, Magistrates, and Town Council of the City of Edinburgh: It seems just like a dream. When a boy I used to read the story of the 'Arabian Nights,' and there was one tale that appealed especially to my fancy and my imagination—the story of Aladdin's Lamp. I imagine that Aladdin's Lamp, with all its beauty, was not half so beautiful as the gift you have presented to me to-day. And this has something which Aladdin's Lamp never possessed. The rubbing of that only gave the material riches of this world. By touching this with eye or hand, I touch the higher qualities of memory, of affection, of all the courtesy that has made my life for four years so enjoyable in this the most beautiful city not only of Europe but of all the world. (Applause.) I said it seemed like a dream. You can imagine how that dream seems intensified when I tell you that it was four years ago, on the 21st day of August, at a quarter to three in the afternoon—the very hour we are here gathered—that the train steamed into the city of Edinburgh bringing myself and family. The four years are completed to a moment. My Lord Provost, in this beautiful gift you have made me re-conjugate the old verb "To Love" which we learned at our mother's lips. I can say "I love" Edinburgh, "I have loved" Edinburgh, "I will love" Edinburgh. (Applause and laughter.) I will go even to the last sentence, that when all is done and completed I can say "I shall have loved," "I will have loved," Edinburgh. (Applause.) I thank you from my heart. I have no words that can adequately express my feeling at this time. You have been too kind to me, all of you. I wish I had a higher eloquence in which to express it; but I shall always cherish, when the twilights gather upon the Catskills, and I look out towards the western hills of beauty on the Hudson—I shall always cherish this hour as the happiest of my life. I thank you, my Lord Provost, Magistrates, and Town Council of Edinburgh. (Loud applause.)

COMPLIMENTARY FAREWELL DINNER

TO HON. WALLACE BRUCE,

U.S. CONSUL, EDINBURGH.

— ——

IN the evening Hon. Wallace Bruce, U.S. Consul of
Edinburgh, was entertained to a public dinner in
the Waterloo Hotel. The Right Honorable the Lord
Provost Russell occupied the chair, and the croupiers
were Bailie Walcot and Mr George Denholm, Argen-
tine Consul (honorary secretary). There were 120
gentlemen present, including the Right Rev. John
Dowden, Bishop of Edinburgh; Rev. Professor Christie,
D.D., of Pennsylvania: Sir William Arrol, Professor
Simpson, Mr Robert Adam, City Chamberlain; Coun-
cillors Pollard, Colston, Gibson, and Cranston; Mr
Henry R. Heath, Chairman of Monument Committee;
Mr Victor Ressich, Spanish Consul; Mr J. W. Tornoe,
Swedish Consul; Mr H. Hansen, Monte Videan Con-
sul; Mr Peter Macdougal, Russian Consul; Hon. Allan
B. Morse, U.S. Consul, Glasgow; Mr Peacock, U.S. Vice

and Deputy, Edinburgh; Mr Richard Lees, U.S. Consular-
Agent, Galashiels; Colonel Woodford, Dr Littlejohn,
Mr John Wilson, Chamber of Commerce; Mr D.
Stevenson, sculptor; Mr W. G. Stevenson, Mr Murray
Lyon, Provost Kinross, Stirling; Rev. George Kirk-
wood, Chaplain to the Forces; Mr M'Leod Fullarton,
John Gifford, Robert Yellowlees, ex-Provost, Stirling;
D. Watson, Hawick; Rev. John Ramsay, Shotts; Mr
W. E. Bartlett, Mr T. Carlaw Martin, Mr Anthony
Watson, Leith; R. Mackay, Leith; Simon Fraser,
Leith; C. L. Forrest, Leith; Robert J. Lindsay, W.S.;
David Paulin, F.R.S.E.; T. F. Kay, New York; John
S. Ferrier, William Brown, Dr Thatcher, Mr John
Ferguson, Linlithgow; Thomas Thomson, Musselburgh;
Robert Anderson, George Square; James Kennedy, D.
Sneddon, Kilmarnock; Robert Scoular, Ayr; Dr Piper,
Philadelphia; Mr J. Scott, Solicitor; Mr Wm. Skinner,
W.S., Town Clerk; ex-Provost Sturrock, Kilmarnock;
Mr Cox of Gorgie; W. Collingridge Barnett; Hon.
Franklin Fairbanks, Vermont; Mr W. J. Murphy,
Arizona; and Mr E. E. Lewis, Sioux City, Iowa.

After dinner the following toasts were proposed and
duly honoured :—

"Her Majesty the Queen;" "The President of the
United States;" "Navy, Army, and Auxiliary Forces;"

" The Guest of the Evening ; " " The Consular Service ; "
" The Clergy."

The LORD PROVOST, in proposing the toast of " The
Guest of the Evening," said—The next toast is the
toast of " The Guest of the Evening "—(loud applause)
—and if I do not speak upon this subject at very great
length, you will understand it is not from any want of
enthusiasm on my part. But you all know that this
is not the first time to-day that Mr Bruce has been
before us, and I think that he himself will be glad
if I speak as briefly and as tersely as I can. But
there are some things I would like to say, and one
of these is that I do not admire the custom in America which throws every good official out of place at
the end of a short administration, and which deprives
us of the services of a valued consul, and of a still
more valued friend, just when we are beginning to
know and appreciate him at his best. (Applause.)
I feel it is a sad thing for us to give Mr Bruce a
farewell dinner, and I am sure we would all be glad
if it were not necessary, and if he were to remain
with us and cultivate the relationships which he has
formed.   When he came to this district four years
ago, he could not come as a stranger, because his
name bewrayed him.   He had to confess himself of

Scottish origin, and we speedily found out that he was worthy of the name which he bears. (Applause.) He associated himself with our life. We always could count upon his kindness and upon his willingness to oblige. Most of us have met him upon public occasions when he put his gift of oratory most freely at the disposal of the public. He has done probably more than any person in this district for long years to cement the friendship which ought to exist, and which does exist, between the Anglo - Saxon race on both sides of the Atlantic. (Applause.) Perhaps, as a literary man by profession, that was easier for him to do than for other people, because, after all, a common literature is the greatest heritage for cementing friendship between two great countries. Mr Bruce, like some others among us, has a passion for the historical and ancient things to be found in our country. We are very glad to have among us Scotsmen as well as Americans who take care to sweep away the dust and keep fresh before our eyes the lessons of times past. Mr Bruce has done this not only in Scotland but in America, and has made many Americans acquainted with Scottish literature of days gone by. He has done this partly by his researches into the literature of times past, and partly by active devotion to that literature himself, and by

c

doing what he could to carry on the story and song of our country and weave it into the song and story of the other side of the Atlantic. (Applause.) To-day I got a confession from him that he means to write about the Yarrow. It is remarkable that most of our poets have found inspiration in running water. In all our leading poets we have constant reference to rivers and streams, and Mr Wallace Bruce has been affected by this also. Many of you have not seen, as I have seen, the beautiful book on the river Hudson of which he is the author, and which does more to bring the river and its beauties before the imagination of those of us who have not seen it in reality than anything else which has been published. (Applause.) We feel grateful to him for his exertions in all these fields, for his good - fellowship, for his kindness and good deeds; and, above all, for doing what he has done to promote the true union of hearts with our American brethren which will make us slow to take cause of offence, and willing rather to wait until we see whether there may not be a different meaning, and willing to accept some reasonable and peaceable way of settling differences rather than fly to angry words and deeds. (Applause.) In proposing the health of Mr Wallace Bruce, I am proposing the health of one who has rendered real services to his own country and to ours, and I put it in that way because he claims his full rights in this country as well as in the United States. I feel sad at the idea that he should leave us; but we live in the hope that, now that he is freed from official duties, we shall soon again see him in this country, and probably his meditations in that other country may enable him to give us some other work. (Applause.) We bid him good-bye and God-speed; we wish him long life and prosperity and success in his literary work, not only for his own sake, but for ourselves, because we hope to enjoy the fruits of his labours.

The toast was honoured with great enthusiasm, the company rising to their feet and singing a few stanzas of " He's a jolly good fellow." Three cheers were also given for Mrs Bruce.

Mr WALLACE BRUCE received a most cordial reception on rising to respond. He said—I desire first to thank the Lord Provost for the words of praise which I feel unmerited, which I would like to attain to, and which I hope, if the years are given me, that I may yet attain to in some measure. I desire also to thank you all for the hearty way in which you have received the toast. I wish also to express my grateful appreciation to many gentlemen at this table for having journeyed long distances, and also to acknowledge the courtesy and kindness of many Edinburgh friends for having taken a day from much-needed vacation to come back to the city and be present here this evening. I desire further to thank Professor Simpson for the toast which he gave, and for the beautiful letter that he has read from a cherished friend—a man well known throughout the United States of America—Professor Drummond. (Applause.) When I studied law in New York with an eloquent advocate, I was given a bit of advice which I have never forgotten. It was that when one had a good subject to talk about he could afford to be happy; but when he had not a very good subject he should be exceedingly dignified. (Laughter.) I am not sure that dignity is at all times indicative of ability; but if I were responding only for this one subject of myself I would attempt to be more dignified than at any previous moment of my life. (Renewed laughter.)

That dignity, however, might be disturbed by the humorous accident of our host's excellent *chef*, who has illuminated the *menu* with Pudding *à la* President Harrison. He evidently has not yet discovered that the "pudding" is now all *à la* Cleveland. (Laughter.)

By some other mistake the toast of the "President

and the Republic," so heartily proposed and eloquently responded to, does not appear on the programme. I am just advised by the Secretary that this is a printer's error; and I am sure that no discourtesy was intended to the Republic or any of its representatives. I desire further to say that President Cleveland is a man with a warm heart. (Applause.) Ten years ago, when Governor of the State of New York, in the presence of 100,000 people, at the Centennial of the Disbanding of the American Army under General Washington at New York, he crossed the platform, with hearty handshake and congratulation, at the close of a poem which I had the honour to deliver. I remember and cherish that greeting. (Applause.) Moreover, whoever is President of the United States of America, no matter what may be our political faith, that man has the love and reverence of every true American. (Applause.)

But to come to the real subject, to the reason why this gathering of friends is here to greet me to-night and bid me a hearty good-bye, and to wish me good fortune in the years that may be given to me and mine in life—to come to that real issue, it is this. I may be able some day to write a poem on " Yarrow." I hope to write something that may stir the hearts of Scottish friends, although I do not know that I may be able fully to do it. I hope to do something for the Hudson and the Catskills, and gather inspiration from the Sierras and the Rocky Mountains. But it is not this that brings you here. It is not what I have done in the past; it is not hope for anything I may do in the future. I believe it is the warm heart of the Scottish people, which overlooks errors or shortcomings when they believe that a man's heart is right. (Applause.) I came here four years ago loving Scotland; I go away loving Scotland more than ever. Twenty-three years ago I walked through your valleys and your Highlands, and I expect to come again to Scotland. (Applause.) I hope to touch sympathetically the Scottish blood that flows in the veins of Americans to-day, worthy descendants of men who helped to lay successfully the corner-stone of the Republic. (Applause.) I think of Alexander Hamilton, born of Scottish parents, going as a lad from the West Indies to become the aide-de-camp of George Washington; I think of Washington Irving, the friend of Sir Walter Scott, a man who loved Edinburgh, and who loved the Tweed, the Avon, and all Britain. (Applause.) If I have been able to do anything in these four years — and I know how humble the work has been — if I have been able to do anything to bind closer together the hearts of the great English-speaking people, I know that I have accomplished more than I could have done in any other direction. There is no reason why the great English-speaking races should not carry their united influence all over the world. I rejoice in the settlement of questions by arbitration. (Applause.) I rejoice in every tie, in every link that binds closer in harmony those great peoples. (Applause.) You, gentlemen, know what Great Britain has done in the past. You may feel that America at times is proud of her institutions, but she is a chip of the old block —(laughter)—and we may well be proud of what the English-speaking race has accomplished. You are proud, and you have a right to be proud, of yourselves and of your children. (Applause.) I thank you, friends, for all the hospitality you have shown me. I carry home to the valley of the Hudson this loving token from the Lord Provost, Magistrates, and Town Council of this beautiful city. I did not need it to make me love Edinburgh and Scotland, but I shall have it before me as a tangible reminder of all you have done for me in the days that are past. (Loud applause.)

The Right Reverend Bishop DOWDEN, of Edinburgh, responding to the toast " The Clergy," said— My Lord Provost, croupiers, and gentlemen, I am

sure I am expressing the sentiments of my learned
brethren as well as my own in saying how grateful
we are for the words used by Mr Paulin, and how
much we appreciate the heartiness with which the
toast has been drunk. But we have come here to-
night not to listen to praise of ourselves, but to express
our respect for the American Consul, and much more
than that, our regard and appreciation of the man, Mr
Wallace Bruce. (Applause.) We appreciate him and
regard him with kindliest feelings for many reasons.
It is an interesting feature, I think more particularly
characteristic of the American Government, that they
very often fill posts in the diplomatic and consular service
with men of distinction in literature. One of the most
memorable evenings I ever spent in this city was one
in which I had a *tête-à-tête* of half an hour with Mr
Russell Lowell. (Applause.) We got on to the subject of literature, and I remember well how he told me
of his interest in the most obscure parts of Scotland,
of which I really knew little or nothing. He had come
to know them because they were mentioned, perhaps
incidentally, in either the poems or novels of Sir Walter
Scott. He knew these novels as well as Mr Bruce, and
that is saying a good deal—(applause)—and he told me
that just the winter before coming here he had suffered
a great loss, and had found a singular source of consola-

tion in the broad open-air feeling of the words of Sir Walter Scott. Sir Walter Scott does not belong to a coterie—he belongs to mankind; and in that broad and healthy atmosphere he found some consolation for a wounded heart, and that very winter he had almost read through the whole works of Sir Walter Scott. There are other examples of men of letters being appointed to posts connected with the diplomatic and consular services, and it was a happy thought on the part of the American Government to send to us one who is a man of letters, and one who is capable. of appreciating the merits of our Scottish men of letters. (Applause.) The clergy are often called in when the banquet of life is over and the lights are about to be put out, and I feel that my observations should be brief. Allow me not only for my brethren, but for every guest, to repeat the words of the poet already recited, which have been taken as the title of Mr Wallace Bruce's latest work—"Here's a Hand." (Loud applause.)

During the evening a number of excellent songs and recitations were given by several gentlemen present, and the gathering broke up after singing a few verses of "Auld Langsyne."

THE STORY OF THE MONUMENT.

From ' Central News.'

IN the summer of 1890, Mrs M'Ewan, widow of a
Scottish-American soldier, called on Mr Wallace
Bruce, United States Consul at Edinburgh, to aid her
in securing a pension from the Government in Washington, as her husband had recently died. The proper
proof was obtained and the pension granted. One
day when she called at the Consulate, Mrs Bruce
chanced to be present, and became interested in her
story : how Sergeant M'Ewan, wearing the blue army
coat with brass buttons, came to the mill in Galashiels
where she was employed, and how, in recesses from
work, little groups would gather about him as he told
incidents of the war. She said she had read ' Uncle
Tom's Cabin,' and the poetry of Whittier, which, she
thought, chimed so sweetly with the songs of Burns.
One day this soldier told the story of his life and won
her. Some years afterwards they came with their
little family to live in Edinburgh. Sickness entered

the household, the father was unable to work. He applied to the Government for a pension, but failed, as he was unable to connect his ailment with exposure on the field. Mrs M‘Ewan told Mrs Bruce how she and her children had worked for five shillings a-week to keep husband and father from the poorhouse, and gave with singular pathos the account of his last illness: how he loved to have the old gun near at hand where he could touch it; how he told the doctor on one of his last visits that he had nothing to give him but his sword, and the kind-hearted doctor replied that it was his business to save life, not to take it, and that he wished neither the sword nor any other recompense but pleasant remembrance, and the wife said, "We will keep the sword for the laddie"; and at last, when the poor soldier, after long months of suffering, died, they found the gun under the coverlet beside him, pressed close to his heart. Mrs Bruce asked where he was buried, that she might go with Mrs M‘Ewan and place some flowers on his grave, although Decoration Day had passed; but the widow answered, with tears in her eyes: "The ground in the common field is all level; I couldna mark the spot. In fact, the next Sabbath after his death I visited it with the bairns, and we found another mourning group had possession. Another body was being buried in the same grave." This story,

told in the beautiful Border language of the Tweed and
the Yarrow, suggested to Consul Wallace Bruce the
idea of a burial-place in Edinburgh for Scottish-
American soldiers. He wrote to several American
friends, and talked with others who visited at the Consulate. All heartily approved of the plan. Some time
afterwards Mr Bruce was walking on the banks of the
Tweed, near Peebles, with Lord Provost Russell, of
Edinburgh. He told Mrs M'Ewan's story, and the
following day wrote a letter to the Lord Provost,
Magistrates, and Town Council, asking for a plot in
one of the city cemeteries. The request was cordially
granted. It then occurred to the Consul that the spot
should be marked with a memorial worthy of the site
in the very heart of the beautiful city. Early in August
Mr Bruce sailed for New York to deliver the Grand
Army Chautauqua Address at the request of Bishop
Vincent, Chancellor of the Chautauqua Assembly,
where over five thousand people, army veterans and
their friends, were gathered, with the late ex-President
Hayes in the chair. It was in this address that Mr
Bruce first publicly announced his idea of a bronze
statue of "Lincoln Freeing the Slave," as a fitting
monument in Great Britain—this being the final act
of Saxon freedom. Mr Henry R. Heath, a veteran and
lifelong friend of the Consul, was present. He entered

heartily into the idea, and was made chairman of the committee of arrangements. Estimates for the monument ranged from six thousand to eight thousand dollars. The contract was awarded to Mr George E. Bissell, a well-known sculptor and. army veteran. Mr Bissell estimated the exact cost of the bronze figures at four thousand dollars, and agreed to furnish them at this price if necessary. The granite work was estimated at about one thousand dollars : proposals came in varying from about one thousand to twenty-four hundred dollars. Messrs Stewart M'Glashen & Son, of Edinburgh, undertook the stone-work and lettering for about nine hundred dollars. Mr Bruce then issued a prospectus with a picture of the proposed monument, and, before taking the steamer for Edinburgh last November, personally saw thirty men who agreed to give one hundred dollars each. During the months of December, January, and February, the amount subscribed reached six thousand dollars, which is gratifying to the Committee, as it enables the sculptor to get some recompense besides fame for his labour. Thus, in ten months after announcement, the work was accomplished, and the monument was unveiled on Monday, 4.30 P.M., August 21st. It is fifteen feet in height, Lincoln in bronze, life-size, with freed slave at his feet, and battle-flags also in bronze, base of polished red Aberdeen granite. Sir William Arrol, a true Scot and a self-made man, such a man as Lincoln would like to have known, was fittingly selected as chairman. A few years since Sir William Arrol was given the freedom of Ayr, and in his speech said, "Thirty years ago I walked through your burgh with my blacksmith tools, asking for work." Hundreds and thousands of Americans to-day look at his great Forth Bridge, a triumph of modern engineering. Mr Bruce, in inviting him, as chairman of the ceremony, fittingly said, "It is the problem of the future to bridge wide oceans and make one family of all nations. Your presence as chairman will rivet another link between our two great English-speaking nations." In the absence of the Honorable Chauncey M. Depew, who had promised to give the address, and fully expected to be present until the last moment, Mr Wallace Bruce presented the monument to the city. It has been a work of love on the part of the United States Consul. The idea was happy, and it has been gracefully executed. It will stand as a monument of love to old Scotia, and will form another link of friendship and goodwill between the nations.

LIST OF SUBSCRIBERS.

EACH of the following gentlemen subscribed one hundred dollars to the undertaking:—

Levi P. Morton,	New York City.
Wm. Walter Phelps,	"
Cornelius Vanderbilt,	"
Andrew Carnegie,	"
Alexander King,	"
Charles Stewart Smith,	"
John S. Kennedy,	"
William Rockefeller,	"
John Sloane,	"
William Clark,	"
J. Pierpont Morgan,	"
E. C. Benedict,	"
James H. Benedict,	"
Wm. Waldorf Astor,	"
Daniel Appleton,	"
Harper & Bros.,	"
J. Kennedy Tod,	"
John B. Dutcher,	"
Solomon Turck,	"
Caledonian Club,	"
Henderson Bros.,	"
Merritt & Ronaldson,	"
David A. Boody,	Brooklyn, N.Y.
John Arbuckle,	"
Henry R. Heath,	"
Francis H. Wilson,	"
Andrew D. Baird,	"

[Over.

Andrew R. Baird, ...	Brooklyn, N.Y.
Alexander S. Baird, ...	"
William W. Baird, ...	"
Joseph Stewart, ...	"
Henry L. Young, ...	Poughkeepsie, N.Y.
Andrew Smith, ...	"
John Donald, ...	"
Wallace Bruce, ...	"
Robert Clark, ...	Chicago, Ill.
Peter M'Ewan, ...	"
A. M. Wright & Co., ...	"
Caledonian Club, ...	"
Geo. Peabody Wetmore, . . .	Newport, R.I.
James Coats, ...	Pawtucket, R.I.
Peter Kinnear, ...	Albany, N.Y.
J. E. Munger, ...	Fishkill, N.Y.
S. D. Coykendall, ...	Rondout, N.Y.
J. Watts de Peyster, ...	Tivoli, N.Y.
Edwin B. Sheldon, ...	Delhi, N.Y.
Geo. E. Lemon, ...	Washington, D.C.
Nathan Bickford, ...	"
R. B. Leuchars, ...	Boston, Mass.
Henry Norwell, ...	"
W. J. Murphy, ...	Phœnix, Arizona.
J. B. White, ...	Ft. Wayne, Ind.
Edward White, ...	"
David C. Bell, ...	Minneapolis, Minn.
Alex. M'Donald, ...	Cincinnati, O.
Lynde Harrison, ...	New Haven, Ct.
John Beattie, ...	Leets Island, Ct.
Thomas Waddell, ...	West Pittston, Pa.
John Young, ...	Jersey City, New Jersey.
Geo. W. Childs, ...	Philadelphia, Pa.
Franklin Fairbanks, ...	St Johnsbury, Vt.
William E. Bartlett, ...	Edinburgh, Scotland.
S. M. Burroughs, ...	London, England.
Total, . .	$6,300.

www.ingramcontent.com/pod-product-compliance
Lightning Source LLC
Chambersburg PA
CBHW031805090426
42739CB00008B/1163